Contents

GAILLARD

C.C.I. CALAIS
904

A tall story

If you've ever been past a **building** site, the chances are you've seen one of the **tallest** machines in the world: a crane. These load **lifters** can also be found in dockyards and factories.

Lift it up...

This type of crane is called a slewing grab.

It's in the name
Cranes are named after another crane – a type of bird. People thought that the machines looked like the birds.

The criss-cross pattern of metal tubes is called a lattice.

Sandhill crane

4

DK Machines at work
CRANE

**LONDON, NEW YORK, MUNICH,
MELBOURNE, and DELHI**

Written and edited by Fleur Star
Designed by Jacqueline Gooden
Publishing manager Susan Leonard
Managing art editor Clare Shedden
Jacket design Hedi Gutt
Jacket editor Mariza O'Keeffe
Jacket copywriter Adam Powley
Picture researcher Liz Moore
Production Emma Hughes
DTP Designer Almudena Díaz
Consultant Alex Dahm

First published in Great Britain in 2005
by Dorling Kindersley Limited
80 Strand, London WC2R 0RL

A Penguin Company

2 4 6 8 10 9 7 5 3 1

Paperback edition
ISBN:13 978-1-4053-1660-6
ISBN:10 1-4053-1660-8

Hardback edition
ISBN:13 978-1-4053-1032-1
ISBN:10 1-4053-1032-4

Colour reproduction by GRB Editrice, S.r.l., Verona, Italy
Printed and bound in China by Toppan Printing Co., Ltd.

Discover more at
www.dk.com

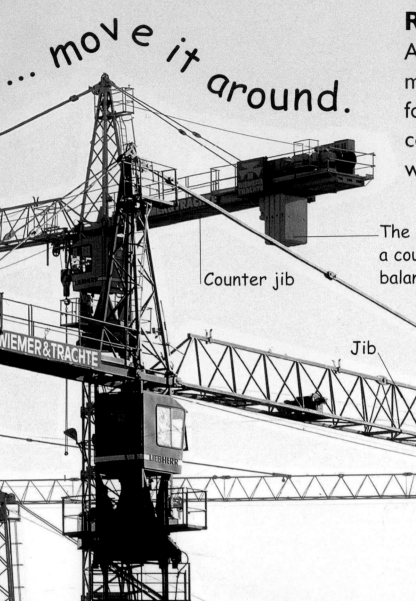

... move it around.

Reach for the sky

All cranes do the same job: they move things that are too heavy for a person to carry. The most common cranes are tower cranes, which look like big T-shapes.

The counter jib has a counterweight to balance the load.

Counter jib

Jib

The long jib carries the heavy load.

On the move

Mobile cranes are not fixed to the ground. They can be folded up and moved from job to job.

WIEMER&TRACHTE

AINSCOUGH
HEAVY CRANE DIVISION

Carry me

Most cranes carry a hook attachment at the end of the cable, to pick up heavy loads.

This crane can reach **20 storeys**.

This crane has a jib on the end of the boom, making it even longer.

Wheely tall

The main part of a hydraulic crane is its boom, the very long **arm** that carries the heavy **load**. When a crane is mounted on a **truck**, it is called a mobile crane.

Going up

A hydraulic boom is like a telescope. It closes up when the crane needs to travel. When on site, fluid is pumped into the boom cylinder, forcing it to extend.

The operator sits way down here.

CRANE SERVICES

CRANE SERVICES

Stand still

The crane cannot balance on its wheels when the boom is extended. Strong metal outriggers are used to keep the crane stable.

TMS870

Making tracks

Not every mobile crane
moves on wheels.
Some use **crawler
tracks**, while others
run on **rails**.

Heave ho... heave ho... heave ho...

It's snow problem
In the Antarctic, cranes with
unusual crawler tracks are
used to move equipment.
The tracks stop the crane
from sinking into the soft snow.

On the rails

Just as trains were invented before cars, the first mobile cranes ran on rails, not roads. Modern railway cranes are used for laying and repairing tracks – and they no longer run on steam!

Tracks are also used on muddy or rough ground.

Under pressure

Crawler tracks spread a crane's weight over a large surface area. If it stood on wheels on soft ground, it would sink.

Towering above

Large **tower** cranes are fixed to the ground to stop them from falling over. The **tallest** free-standing crane stood **122 m** (400 ft) from hook to ground.

Swinging high

Saddle jib, or T-shaped, tower cranes move their loads by swinging their jibs around in a circle. This is called slewing.

Taller towers are tied to buildings for support.

Being at the top

Where space is tight, tower cranes with luffing jibs are used. These jibs move up and down as well as swing round.

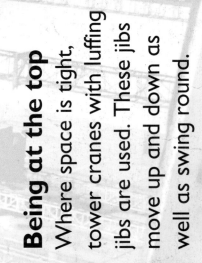

In control

A tower crane **operator** needs a good head for **heights**. Sitting high up in the crane's cab, the operator **controls** the movement of the jib.

Do look down

The crane operator needs to be able to see the load, which hangs below the trolley that runs along the jib. The cab turns with the jib to follow its swing.

Watch

out below!

Climbing frame
Tall towers have hoists that lift an operator up to the cab. But those who work on shorter cranes face a long climb up a ladder.

Lifting works

Mobile cranes and tower cranes are useful **outdoors**, but what happens when heavy goods need to be moved inside **factories**?

Off the wall
Jib cranes can be fixed to the wall or bolted to the floor like this one. The top arm, or jib, rotates to move the load.

The trolley rolls along on rails called girders.

Gird your strength

Some factories have girder cranes that run on rails near the roof. The crane's trolley scoots between the stockpiles and the trucks.

Unusual loads are carried on special kinds of hook attachments.

On the water

Floating cranes can be found on ships and barges that need to move heavy objects. Some ships are specially built with cranes on deck. Others might carry mobile cranes.

Take a dive

The *Keldysh* is the world's biggest research ship. Here its crane lowers a submarine into the sea. The people aboard are going to study the wreck of the *Titanic*.

Need a lift?

This massive lattice crane actually floats aboard a boat. It is used to raise sunken ships or tow broken-down ships safely back to shore.

Main attraction

Most cranes have hooks to carry their loads, but this crane has electro-magnetic pads. These strong magnets "stick" to the steel submarine.

Freight lifters

The cranes at this **freight** terminal are used to load massive **containers** onto ships, ready for exporting overseas.

These stairs lead to the control cab.

Trolley dash

The crane's load hangs down from a trolley, which sits on the boom below the cab.

The trolley carries its load towards the ship.

Container cranes are also used to unload ships.

A long reach
These cranes are ship-to-shore container cranes. The towers are lined up in a long row, and jut out over the edge of the docks to reach the ships.

Fast work
Before cranes, it could take weeks to load and unload freight from ships. Now it takes hours.

All at sea

Offshore crane vessels are the world's biggest cranes. These huge **floating** machines are important to the **oil** industry, as they help to build oil rigs.

This offshore crane vessel is based on the same design as an oil rig.

Load of goods

Oil rig platforms are high above the sea's surface, so cranes are used to lift aboard supplies from boats. The boats get tossed around on the waves, so the cranes have to move fast to hook the load.

Carried aboard

It's not just supplies that arrive by crane: even the rig workers are lifted aboard from their boats. This is dangerous in rough seas.

Weighed down

Offshore crane vessels can lift oil rig parts that weigh thousands of tonnes (tons). The vessels use lots of anchors to stop them moving about when working.

Log loads

You can't get wood without trees, but how do you get the trees from the **forests** to the **logging mills?**

The crane's grapple picks up logs just like you would pick up a bunch of pencils.

These pine tree logs could be used to make furniture.

Run of the mill
This gantry crane is similar to the ones seen at the docks. It has a big frame with a trolley that runs back and forth over the pile of logs below.

Pile 'em up

Once the trees have been felled, they need to be quickly piled onto trucks. This loader crane is just like an extra-strong, extended arm.

Bring your own

Some logging trucks have their own inbuilt hydraulic loader cranes. The crane is controlled from its base, just behind the truck's cab.

Helping hand

Lifting concrete **blocks** is all
in a day's work for many cranes.
But these machines can perform
much more **unusual** tasks.
Some are even out of this world!

Watch this space
An astronaut on a space
walk is tied to a type of
crane. It pushes him
around in space.

This arm connects to the
space shuttle's orbiter.

A green crane?
A crane helps with an environmental project by
lowering an old plane into the sea. The wreck
will create a reef, for fish and plants to live on.

The crane is
called a Space
Shuttle Remote
Manipulator System.

24

There's no land to
walk on out here...

Moving house?
Not every house is built where it stands. This log cabin was made in a factory and transported by lorry. It needs a crane to lower it into place.

Up for grabs

The **hook** on the end of a crane is very useful for lifting blocks, but how do you lift **mud** or even **people?**

People in the basket are tied in for safety.

Caged in
A personnel basket is used to carry people. The crane lifts them up to work in places they could not otherwise reach.

Spreader: this large clamp fits on top of a container. It is often used at the docks.

"Orange peel" grab: the grab's fingers close tightly to stop the load escaping.

Electromagnet: this powerful magnet will attract iron from a pile of scrap metal.

A dragline bucket is mainly used in mining.

It's a drag

This heavy scoop is called a dragline bucket. The crane pulls the bucket along the ground. Cranes that use these buckets are shorter and stronger than those that lift loads.

Days of old

Cranes are not a new idea. **Lifting machines** were used in ancient Egypt and Greece more than **2,000 years** ago.

People power
Ancient cranes were not powered by electricity or steam: they used people. Slaves had to turn the wheels, which lifted the load.

Large cranes today use wire ropes rather than chains for lifting.

The size of the man gives an idea of how big the crane and its load are.

CALLOWA

AUK

Full steam ahead

This 100-year-old crane runs on rails and is powered by steam. Despite its age, it is still being used in India today.

Is anybody home?

Many steam cranes had large machinery houses – the case over a crane's workings. This one from 1900 looks like a house.

It's a fact

All cranes used to be made of wood. The first non-wooden crane was made of cast iron, in 1834.

The first steam crane was invented in 1839. Before then, a crane was powered by an animal on a treadmill or by a person turning a crank.

Picture gallery

Crawler tracks

These tracks stop the crane from slipping or sinking in the snow. Crawlers are mainly used on rough or muddy ground.

Loader crane

Hydraulic loader cranes are often mounted on trucks, but they can also be fitted on board ships.

Slewing grab

This crane, used in docks, has a double boom so it can lift heavier loads.

Mobile crane

This 18-wheel truck bears a crane that can extend 50 m (164 ft) – taller than eight giraffes.

Tower crane

The world's biggest tower crane, the K10000, can lift 120 tonnes (117 tons) – that's 25 elephants!

Dragline crane

Dragging a bucket over the ground is a different action from the usual lifting of loads.

Jib crane

Some factories have whole rooms full of these cranes – one at every workstation.

Spreader

This clamp is one of many crane attachments. Others include buckets for molten metal and suckers for glass.

Steam crane

Early steam cranes ran on rails. The first steam crane to drive freely, like a car, was invented in 1868.

Gantry crane

Gantries can have solid or lattice legs and beams. The first lattice was used in 1874, and is also used in other types of crane.

Glossary

Boom a crane's long, extending arm.

Counter jib the arm of a tower crane that is opposite the jib. The counterweight and motors sit here.

Counterweight a metal or concrete block attached to a crane, which balances the load to stop the crane from falling over.

Crane a machine that is used to lift items too heavy be moved by hand.

Crawler tracks a metal belt around a set of wheels on a machine, which helps it move over rough, soft, or slippery ground.

Freight goods that are transported to be sold.

Gantry a big frame that can be used to support a crane. Its bridge shape is designed to reach over obstacles.

Girder a strong, main support in a roof or other structure.

Hydraulics a system of operating machinery that uses fluid to push pistons to make the machine work.

Jib the arm of a crane that carries the load.

Lattice the criss-cross pattern of metal bars that makes up a strong frame – but one that is lighter than solid metal.

Luffing the action of raising or lowering the angle of a boom or jib.

Outriggers the metal legs that support a mobile crane.

Slewing the action of moving a jib in a circle.

Trolley the part of a crane that runs along the jib. It has a hook attached to carry the load.

Index

Mobile crane

Acknowledgements

Dorling Kindersley would like to thank: Mechan Limited Sheffield for use of jib crane image, and Sarah Mills for picture library services.

Picture credits:

The publisher would like to thank the following for their kind permission to reproduce their photographs:

t = top, b = bottom, l = left, c = centre, bgd = background

AKG Images 28cl; Alamy Images/Pictures Colour Library 4-5 bgd, /Leslie Garland 9b, /Maximilian Weinzierl 10-11, /Bo Jansson 25b, /Rolf Adlercreutz 26tl, /Pixoi Ltd 26bc, /David Jackson 30br; Alvey & Tower 14-15; Construction Photography/ Damian Gillie 1, /Anthony Weller 2-3, /Chris Henderson 6-7, 6t, /P.G. Bowater 11b; Corbis UK/Richard Cummins 7b, /Ecoscene/Graham Neden 8-9, 30tl, /Bob Krist 12-13, /Ralph White 16-17, 17t, /SABA/Tom Wagner 18-19, /Joel W. Rogers 18b, /Steve Chenn 21tr, /ChromoSohm Inc/Joseph Sohm 23tl, 30tr, /Amos Nachoum 24l, /Colin Garratt 29t, 31bl; Dorling Kindersley Media Library/Richard Leeney 5b, 30bc, 32; Getty Images/Robert Harding Picture Library/Mark Chivers 4l, 30bl, /Stone/James Wells 20l, /Christian Lagereek 31br, /Image Bank/Terie Rakke 22-23, /Michael Melford 22l, /Harald Sund 26br, /Photographer's Choice/Sandra Baker 26bl, 31tr; Robert Harding Picture Library/Premium Stock 19R; Mechan Limited Sheffield (www.mechan.co.uk), courtesy 14l, 31tc; QA Photos/ Jim Bryne 9t; Reuters/Kin Cheung 13t, Cheryl Hatch 16b; Science and Society Picture Library/National Railway Museum 28-29; Science Photo Library/Peter Chadwick 4bc, /NASA 24-25; Zefa Visual Media UK Ltd/E. Streichan 20-21, /Masterfile/Mike Dobel 26-27, 31tl.

All other images © Dorling Kindersley
For further information see: www.dkimages.com